THE BEST MLB
OUTFIELDERS
OF ALL TIME

By Bo Smolka

Published by ABDO Publishing Company, PO Box 398166, Minneapolis, MN 55439. Copyright © 2014 by Abdo Consulting Group, Inc. International copyrights reserved in all countries. No part of this book may be reproduced in any form without written permission from the publisher. SportsZone™ is a trademark and logo of ABDO Publishing Company.

Printed in the United States of America,
North Mankato, Minnesota
092013
012014
♻ THIS BOOK CONTAINS AT LEAST 10% RECYCLED MATERIALS.

Editor: Chrös McDougall
Series Designer: Christa Schneider

Photo credits: AP Images, cover (left), 1 (left), 7, 9, 11, 13, 15, 17, 19, 21, 23, 27, 31, 33, 35, 37, 39, 41; Kathy Willens/AP Images, cover (right), 1 (right); Harry Harris/AP Images, 25; Joe Holloway, Jr./AP Images, 29; Eric Risberg/AP Images, 43; Gene Puskar/AP Images, 45, 53; Jim Mone/AP Images, 47; Rusty Kennedy/AP Images, 49; Julie Jacobson/AP Images, 51; Gary Stewart/AP Images, 55; Charles Krupa/AP Images, 57; John Froschauer/AP Images, 59; Frank Franklin II/AP Images, 61

Library of Congress Control Number: 2013945895

Cataloging-in-Publication Data
Smolka, Bo.
 The best MLB outfielders of all time / Bo Smolka.
   p. cm. -- (Major League Baseball's best ever)
Includes bibliographical references and index.
ISBN 978-1-62403-116-8
1. Major League Baseball (Organization)--Juvenile literature. 2. Fielding (Baseball)--Juvenile literature. 3. Outfielders (Baseball)--Juvenile literature. I. Title.
796.357--dc23

                                        2013945895

TABLE OF CONTENTS

Introduction   4
Tris Speaker   6
Joe DiMaggio   10
Mickey Mantle   14
Willie Mays   18
Al Kaline   22
Hank Aaron   26
Roberto Clemente   30
Frank Robinson   34
Carl Yastrzemski   38
Rickey Henderson   42
Kirby Puckett   46
Barry Bonds   50
Ken Griffey Jr.   54
Ichiro Suzuki   58

Honorable Mentions   62
Glossary   63
For More Information   63
Index   64
About the Author   64

INTRODUCTION

From the time the first baseball field was laid out, fast, athletic players have covered the ground in the outfield.

Major League Baseball's (MLB's) best outfielders produce a lot of runs with their offense, and they take away a lot of runs with their defense. They use their speed to chase down fly balls in the gap. They make diving catches worthy of the highlight reel. They make long, strong, accurate throws back to the infield. And they leap high at the fence, turning would-be home runs into outs. Great outfielders prove that baseball is not just about hitting home runs. Amazing defense can be just as exciting.

Here are some of the best outfielders in MLB history.

TRIS SPEAKER

Tris Speaker was ready. It was 1914. The Boston Red Sox's center fielder was at home in Fenway Park. And Detroit Tigers base runner Harry Heilmann was taking a lead off of second base. As the batter smacked a line drive, Heilmann took off for third base. He was hoping to score.

Speaker, however, had other plans. He charged in and caught the sinking line drive in the air. He then kept running in the direction of second base. He beat Heilmann to the base for an unassisted double play.

Speaker had six unassisted double plays in his career. That is a record for an outfielder. He was a master at getting a good jump on the ball and making a catch. He could also fire a strong throw back to the infield. He was involved in 139 outfield double plays during his career—another record.

Tris Speaker was one of baseball's first great star players.

Speaker also was one of the best hitters to ever swing a bat. He hit better than .300 in 18 of his 19 full major league seasons. His career average of .345 was still sixth best in MLB history through 2013.

Home runs were not common in Speaker's era. But he pounded the ball. He led the league in doubles eight times. In 1912, Speaker led the American League (AL) in doubles (53) and home runs (10). He also was the AL Most Valuable Player (MVP) that season. Speaker's total of 792 doubles was still a major league record through 2013.

Speaker became a successful manager for the Cleveland Indians while he was still playing. In 1920, Speaker hit .388 with 50 doubles and also managed the team to a World Series championship.

448

The number of outfield assists Speaker had during his career—a major league record through 2013.

Tris Speaker, *center*, poses with Boston Red Sox outfielders Duffy Lewis, *left*, and Harry Hooper.

TRIS SPEAKER

Hometown: Hubbard, Texas

Height, Weight: 5 feet 11, 193 pounds

Birth Date: April 4, 1888

Teams: Boston Americans/Red Sox (1907–15)
   Cleveland Indians (1916–26)
   Washington Senators (1927)
   Philadelphia Athletics (1928)

MVP Award: 1912

JOE DIMAGGIO

The New York Yankees were in trouble. They were trailing the New York Giants two games to one in the 1951 World Series, and they needed a spark. They got it from outfielder Joe DiMaggio. He drilled a two-run home run, leading the Yankees to a 6–2 win. The Yankees went on to win the World Series for the third straight year.

DiMaggio was part of a Yankees dynasty. In 13 seasons, he helped lead the Yankees to the World Series 10 times. They won nine of them. And DiMaggio, who was a graceful, quick outfielder and tremendous hitter, was one of the main reasons.

As a rookie in 1936, DiMaggio batted .323 and was outstanding in center field.

Joe DiMaggio became known as "The Yankee Clipper" during his famous career with the New York Yankees.

Yankee Stadium at that time had huge power alleys. The fence in left-center and center field was more than 450 feet (137 m) from home plate. That is farther than any major league stadium today. Outfielders had to range far and wide to track down fly balls. And they had to make strong, accurate throws back to the infield. It was a difficult job, but DiMaggio made it look easy.

He did that with his batting, too. DiMaggio hit better than .300 11 times during his career. He had more than 100 runs batted in (RBIs) seven years in a row. And he might have done even more, but he missed three seasons while serving in the military during World War II.

"There was never a day when I was as good as Joe DiMaggio at his best," Hall of Fame player Stan Musial once said. "Joe was the best, the very best I ever saw."

56

The number of consecutive games in which DiMaggio recorded a hit in 1941. As of 2013, that was still a major league record.

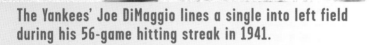

The Yankees' Joe DiMaggio lines a single into left field during his 56-game hitting streak in 1941.

JOE DIMAGGIO

Hometown: Martinez, California

Height, Weight: 6 feet 2, 193 pounds

Birth Date: November 25, 1914

Team: New York Yankees (1936–42, 1946–51)*

All-Star Games: 1936, 1937, 1938, 1939, 1940, 1941, 1942, 1946, 1947, 1948, 1949, 1950, 1951

MVP Awards: 1939, 1941, 1947

* Did not play 1943–45 because of military service

MICKEY MANTLE

New York Yankees pitcher Don Larsen had been perfect. Center fielder Mickey Mantle made sure he stayed that way. In the fifth inning in Game 5 of the 1956 World Series, Mantle sprinted hard to the gap in deep left-center field. He reached out and took away a hit from the Brooklyn Dodgers. That catch preserved Larsen's perfect game. Through 2012, it was still the only perfect game in World Series history.

"Mantle made such a beautiful catch," Larsen said years later. "That ball probably would have been a home run in most parks."

New York Yankees center fielder Mickey Mantle, *left*, reaches to make a catch during the 1962 World Series.

The Yankees went on to win the World Series in 1956. Mantle won the AL Triple Crown that season. He led the league in batting average (.353), home runs (52), and RBIs (130). After Mantle, there were only two Triple Crown winners in the major leagues in the next 55 years.

18

The number of home runs Mantle hit in the World Series during his career. That remained a record through 2013.

Yankees fans got used to big things from Mantle. With him patrolling the outfield, the Yankees went to the World Series 12 times in 14 seasons from 1951 to 1964. They won the World Series seven times in that span.

Mantle also could crush the ball. The powerful switch-hitter led the AL in home runs four times. He led the league in runs five times. And he hit .300 or better 10 times. As he proved time and again, Mantle could win games with both his glove and his bat.

The Yankees' Mickey Mantle hits a grand slam against the Brooklyn Dodgers during Game 5 of the 1953 World Series.

MICKEY MANTLE

Hometown: Spavinaw, Oklahoma

Height, Weight: 5 feet 11, 195 pounds

Birth Date: October 20, 1931

Team: New York Yankees (1951–68)

All-Star Games: 1952, 1953, 1954, 1955, 1956, 1957, 1958, 1959, 1960, 1961, 1962, 1963, 1964, 1965, 1967, 1968

Gold Glove: 1962

MVP Awards: 1956, 1957, 1962

WILLIE MAYS

It was Game 1 of the 1954 World Series.
The score was tied in the eighth inning. The Cleveland Indians had runners on first and second base with nobody out. But the New York Giants had center fielder Willie Mays.

Indians first baseman Vic Wertz hammered a pitch. Mays ran full speed toward the wall. The ball kept carrying. But Mays kept running to the deepest part of the Polo Grounds. Then he looked over his left shoulder and saw the ball finally coming down. Approximately 450 feet (137 m) from home plate, Mays reached out and caught the ball with his back to the rest of the field. He immediately spun around and threw the ball like a laser to second base. The famous play showed the speed and arm strength that made Mays one of the greatest outfielders of all time. And it helped the Giants win that game and the World Series.

New York Giants outfielder Willie Mays makes his famous catch during Game 1 of the 1954 World Series.

Mays began his career with the Birmingham Black Barons in the Negro Leagues. He then spent time in the minor leagues. Mays joined the Giants as a 20-year-old in 1951. He was the National League (NL) Rookie of the Year that season. Mays had trouble remembering names, so he would greet people with, "Say, hey!" He soon became known as the "Say Hey Kid."

In 1955, Mays led the NL in home runs (51) and triples (13). He finished his career with a .302 batting average and 660 home runs. Through 2013, that was the fourth-most in history. Plus he won 12 Gold Gloves in his career, showcasing his versatility.

"If there ever were a baseball god, it would be him," former NL president Bill White once said. "Nobody could play like he could. Nobody."

24

The number of All-Star Games in which Mays played. That was tied for the most all time through 2013. (There were two All-Star Games held each year from 1959 to 1962.)

Willie Mays became one of baseball's all-around greatest players during his long career, spent mostly with the Giants.

WILLIE MAYS

Hometown: Westfield, Alabama

Height, Weight: 5 feet 10, 170 pounds

Birth Date: May 6, 1931

Teams: New York/San Francisco Giants (1951–52, 1954–72)* New York Mets 1972–73)

All-Star Games: 1954–73

Gold Gloves: 1957–68

MVP Awards: 1954, 1965

Rookie of the Year: 1951

* Did not play in 1953 because of military service

AL KALINE

The ball was lined into the right-field corner. Detroit Tigers right fielder Al Kaline raced over and fielded the ball near the wall. He quickly spun around to his left. Without even looking first, he fired a strike to second base. The surprised batter thought he had a double, but he instead was tagged out.

That spin and throw became a signature play for Kaline. In fact, the right field corner at Tigers Stadium became known as "Kaline's Corner."

Kaline patrolled right field for the Tigers for more than 20 years. He was so popular that he became known as "Mr. Tiger."

Al Kaline played 22 seasons for the Detroit Tigers and helped them win the 1968 World Series.

Kaline made the major leagues as an 18-year-old in 1953. From 1955 to 1967, he was an All-Star every season. His play in right field also earned him seven straight Gold Gloves and 10 total.

In 1968, Kaline missed a month with a broken arm after a pitch hit him. But he returned to help lead the Tigers to the World Series title. In the World Series, Kaline hit .379 with two home runs.

Kaline ended his career with 3,007 hits and 399 home runs. Mr. Tiger was definitely one of the best.

"He could hit, he could run, he could field, and he could throw," longtime Tigers radio announcer Ernie Harwell said. "And I don't think I've ever seen a right fielder more adept at going over in the corner, grabbing that ball on a bounce, and turning and firing to second base."

20

Kaline's age when he hit .340 and won the AL batting title in 1955. Through 2013, he was the youngest batting champion.

Tigers right fielder Al Kaline snags a would-be home run by the New York Yankees' Mickey Mantle during a 1958 game.

AL KALINE

Hometown: Baltimore, Maryland

Height, Weight: 6 feet 1, 175 pounds

Birth Date: December 19, 1934

Team: Detroit Tigers (1953–74)

All-Star Games: 1955, 1956, 1957, 1958, 1959, 1960, 1961, 1962, 1963, 1964, 1965, 1966, 1967, 1971, 1974

Gold Gloves: 1957, 1958, 1959, 1961, 1962, 1963, 1964, 1965, 1966, 1967

HANK
AARON

The score was tied in the 11th inning on September 23, 1957. The Milwaukee Braves needed a big play. As usual, Hank Aaron was there to deliver it. He stepped up to bat and slammed a home run. That clinched the pennant for the Braves. The crowd went wild. And Aaron's teammates carried him off the field.

Aaron went on to lead the Braves to the 1957 World Series title. He batted .393 with three home runs in the Fall Classic. Milwaukee beat the New York Yankees in seven games.

Aaron began his amazing career in the Negro Leagues. He joined the Braves in 1954 at age 20 and played 23 seasons in the majors.

Hank Aaron became baseball's home run king over a long, consistent career spent mostly with the Braves.

Aaron is most famous for breaking Babe Ruth's career home run record. Aaron finished with 755 home runs. That record stood for 33 years.

Aaron was not just a big home run hitter, though. He was what baseball scouts call a "five-tool player." That means he could hit for average, hit for power, throw, catch, and run very well. Plus he was consistent. Aaron batted .305 in his career and twice led the NL in hitting. He stole 31 bases in 1963. And as an outfielder, he used his speed to track down fly balls. He had 17 assists as a right fielder in 1956. After a while, runners stopped trying to run on Aaron and his powerful arm.

"In the '50s, when you watched Hank Aaron, you knew you were watching something really special," MLB commissioner Bud Selig said.

2,297

The number of RBIs Aaron had in his career. That was still a major league record through 2013.

The Braves' Hank Aaron hits his 715th career home run on April 8, 1974, to break Babe Ruth's career home run record.

HANK AARON

Hometown: Mobile, Alabama

Height, Weight: 6 feet, 180 pounds

Birth Date: February 5, 1934

Teams: Milwaukee/Atlanta Braves (1954–74)
Milwaukee Brewers (1975–76)

All-Star Games: 1955, 1956, 1957, 1958, 1959, 1960, 1961, 1962, 1963, 1964, 1965, 1966, 1967, 1968, 1969, 1970, 1971, 1972, 1973, 1974, 1975

Gold Gloves: 1958, 1959, 1960

MVP Award: 1957

ROBERTO CLEMENTE

Roberto Clemente smacked the pitch high and deep to left field. When it finally landed beyond the left-field fence, the Pittsburgh Pirates led Game 7 of the 1971 World Series 1–0.

The Pirates went on to win 2–1 to take the World Series over the favored Baltimore Orioles. Clemente was the star. He hit .414 in the World Series with two home runs.

Clemente was one of the best hitters of his generation. His lifetime average was .317. But as good as he was at hitting, he might have been even better defensively. Clemente had one of the strongest throwing arms in baseball history. He won 12 straight Gold Gloves for his play in right field for the Pirates. And he routinely threw strikes of 300 feet (91 m) or more from right field to the catcher at home plate.

Pittsburgh Pirates outfielder Roberto Clemente was a star both at the plate and in the field.

Longtime broadcaster Vin Scully once said, "Clemente could field the ball in New York and throw out a guy in Pennsylvania."

Clemente was born in Puerto Rico. He became an idol to thousands of young Latin American players in the 1950s and 1960s. Clemente finished his career with 3,000 hits. But his career ended abruptly at age 38.

In 1972, an earthquake hit Nicaragua. Clemente organized a trip to take supplies to that country. But his plane crashed on December 31, 1972, and he was killed. From then on MLB has given out an annual Roberto Clemente Award. It goes to someone who is an excellent player and also does a lot of positive work in the community. It is a fitting tribute to one of baseball's best.

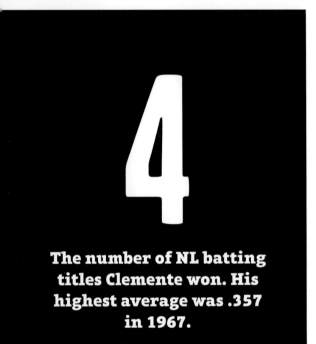

4

The number of NL batting titles Clemente won. His highest average was .357 in 1967.

The Pirates' Roberto Clemente robs a New York Mets batter of a hit during a 1970 game.

ROBERTO CLEMENTE

Hometown: Carolina, Puerto Rico

Height, Weight: 5 feet 11, 175 pounds

Birth Date: August 18, 1934

Team: Pittsburgh Pirates (1955–72)

All-Star Games: 1960, 1961, 1962, 1963, 1964, 1965, 1966, 1967, 1969, 1970, 1971, 1972

Gold Gloves: 1961, 1962, 1963, 1964, 1965, 1966, 1967, 1968, 1969, 1970, 1971, 1972

MVP Award: 1966

FRANK ROBINSON

Baltimore Orioles outfielder Frank Robinson sent the ball towering toward the fence. It sailed way over the left fielder's head. It sailed over the fans sitting in the left-field seats. And as stunned fans watched, the ball sailed right out of the stadium! Robinson became the only player ever to hit a home run out of Baltimore's Memorial Stadium.

That home run showed the kind of strength that made Robinson one of baseball's greatest players in the 1950s and 1960s. He was feared as a hitter, but he also was a solid outfielder. He was aggressive to the ball and had a strong arm.

Robinson broke into the majors with the Cincinnati Reds in 1956. He was named the NL Rookie of the Year that season.

Outfielder Frank Robinson was one of MLB's best hitters from the 1950s to the 1970s.

In 1961, he was named the NL MVP.

He hit .323 with 37 home runs and 124 RBIs that season in leading the Reds to the pennant.

In 1965, Robinson turned 30. The Reds' general manager did not think Robinson would be very good much longer. So the Reds traded Robinson to the Orioles before the 1966 season. It turned out that Robinson had a lot of good years left.

In his first season in Baltimore, Robinson won the AL Triple Crown. He led the league in batting (.316), home runs (49), and RBIs (122). And he was again named the MVP. That made Robinson the only player to have been named MVP in both leagues through 2013. He also led the Orioles to the World Series four times.

Robinson later became the first African-American manager in the major leagues.

586

The number of home runs Robinson hit in his 21-year career. When he retired, that ranked fourth in major league history.

The Baltimore Orioles' Frank Robinson hits his 499th career home run during a 1971 game against the Detroit Tigers.

FRANK ROBINSON

Hometown: Beaumont, Texas

Height, Weight: 6 feet 1, 183 pounds

Birth Date: August 31, 1935

Teams: Cincinnati Reds (1956–65)
Baltimore Orioles (1966–71)
Los Angeles Dodgers (1972)
California Angels (1973–74)
Cleveland Indians (1974–76)

All-Star Games: 1956, 1957, 1959, 1961, 1962,
1965, 1966, 1967, 1969, 1970, 1971, 1974

Gold Glove: 1958

MVP Awards: 1961, 1966

Rookie of the Year: 1956

CARL YASTRZEMSKI

The 1967 pennant race was one of the best of all time. Late in the season, four teams were in a tight battle for the AL title. Then Carl Yastrzemski of the Boston Red Sox took control.

In Boston's last 12 games, "Yaz," as he was known, hit .523 with five home runs and 16 RBIs. The Red Sox needed to beat the Minnesota Twins in the last two games of the season to win the pennant. And they did. In those two games, Yastrzemski was 7-for-8 with one home run and six RBIs.

"There are some people who think Carl Yastrzemski's last two weeks of the 1967 . . . season were the best two weeks that any baseball player ever had," baseball writer Daniel Okrent said.

The Boston Red Sox's Carl Yastrzemski holds the ball he hit for his 3,000th career hit in 1979.

Yastrzemski won the AL Triple Crown that season. He batted .326 with 44 home runs and 121 RBIs.

Yastrzemski also was one of the finest left fielders of all time. The left field wall at Boston's Fenway Park is known as the Green Monster.

It stands more than 37 feet (11.3 m) high. And Yastrzemski played that wall as well as anyone ever has. Sometimes, he would field a ball high off the wall and fire it back to second base, often throwing out the hitter trying for a double. Other times, he would jump and make catches, crashing into the Green Monster.

Yastrzemski hit plenty of baseballs over walls himself. He was the first AL player with 3,000 hits and 400 home runs.

3

The number of times Yastrzemski led the AL in batting average. It is also the number of seasons in which Yastrzemski hit 40 or more home runs.

Boston's Carl Yastrzemski leaps high over the left-field fence to steal a home run during the 1969 All-Star Game.

CARL YASTRZEMSKI

Hometown: Southampton, New York

Height, Weight: 5 feet 11, 175 pounds

Birth Date: August 22, 1939

Team: Boston Red Sox (1961–83)

All-Star Games: 1963, 1965, 1966, 1967, 1968, 1969, 1970, 1971, 1972, 1973, 1974, 1975, 1976, 1977, 1978, 1979, 1982, 1983

Gold Gloves: 1963, 1965, 1967, 1968, 1969, 1971, 1977

MVP Award: 1967

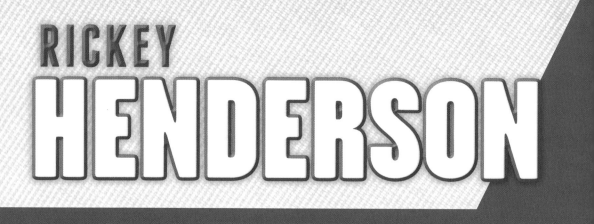

RICKEY HENDERSON

Rickey Henderson took his lead off second base. He bounced on the balls of his feet, twitched his fingers, and watched the pitcher. As the pitcher started his delivery toward home plate, Henderson took off toward third base. He dove headfirst, sliding his hands into the base before the throw from the catcher arrived. Henderson had just stolen the 939th base of his career. That set a major league record.

Henderson was one of the fastest players of his generation. As a left fielder, that helped him get to balls hit in the gaps or down the line.

As good as his fielding was, though, Henderson will always be known for his base stealing.

Rickey Henderson of the Oakland Athletics celebrates after stealing his record 939th base during a 1991 game.

He stole 130 bases in 1982. That was still a modern MLB record in 2013. Henderson led the major leagues in stolen bases 12 times. He finished his career with 1,406 stolen bases. Through 2013, no one else in baseball history even had 1,000.

Henderson was the ideal leadoff hitter. He was good with his bat. And with a crouched stance, he drew a lot of walks. Then once he was on base, he was *really* trouble for the other team. Henderson often stole second and sometimes third. That put him in great position to score when a teammate got a hit. Through 2013, Henderson held the major league record for runs in a career (2,295).

Henderson played for nine teams during his 21-year career. He won the World Series with the Oakland Athletics and the Toronto Blue Jays. Henderson played in the majors until he was 44. And he never stopped running.

81

The number of home runs Henderson hit as the leadoff hitter to begin a game. Through 2013, that was a major league record.

Oakland's Rickey Henderson slides ahead of the throw for a steal during a 1989 game against the Toronto Blue Jays.

RICKEY HENDERSON

Hometown: Chicago, Illinois

Height, Weight: 5 feet 10, 180 pounds

Birth Date: December 25, 1958

Teams: Oakland Athletics (1979–84; 1989–93; 1994–95; 1998); New York Yankees (1985–89); Toronto Blue Jays (1993); San Diego Padres (1996–97, 2001); Anaheim Angels (1997); New York Mets (1999–2000); Seattle Mariners (2000); Boston Red Sox (2002); LA Dodgers (2003)

All-Star Games: 1980, 1982–88, 1990, 1991

Gold Glove: 1981

MVP Award: 1990

Silver Sluggers: 1981, 1985, 1990

KIRBY PUCKETT

Crack!

The ball was hit high and deep to center field. Minnesota Twins center fielder Kirby Puckett drifted back to the warning track. He kept his eyes on the ball as he neared the wall. Then, like a cat, he leaped up in the air. With his left arm and glove extended, Puckett reached way up as he bounced against the wall. He caught the ball for an out.

The home crowd at the Metrodome in Minneapolis went wild. But Puckett was not yet done in Game 6 of the 1991 World Series. With the game tied in the bottom of the 11th inning, Puckett forced Game 7 with a walk-off home run. The Twins won the World Series the next night.

Minnesota Twins center fielder Kirby Puckett celebrates after his walk-off home run in Game 6 of the 1991 World Series.

Puckett was one of the best defensive outfielders of the 1980s and 1990s. He also was a fantastic hitter. And when the games mattered most, Puckett was at his best.

Puckett was always one of the shortest players on his team. He was only 5 feet, 8 inches tall. But he had thick, powerful legs. That helped him get tremendous height when he jumped at the fence to take away home runs from opposing hitters.

Puckett led the AL in batting in 1989 with a .339 average. He had more than 200 hits four times in his career. And he won a Gold Glove six times in seven years.

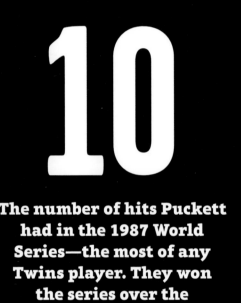

10

The number of hits Puckett had in the 1987 World Series—the most of any Twins player. They won the series over the St. Louis Cardinals in seven games.

Unfortunately, Puckett's career was cut short. He had to retire at age 36 after he lost vision in one eye. But by then, Puckett had already established himself as one of the best outfielders of all time.

The Twins' Kirby Puckett watches his hit sail for a home run during the 1987 playoffs.

KIRBY PUCKETT

Hometown: Chicago, Illinois

Height, Weight: 5 feet 8, 178 pounds

Birth Date: March 14, 1960

Team: Minnesota Twins (1984–95)

All-Star Games: 1986, 1987, 1988, 1989, 1990, 1991, 1992, 1993, 1994, 1995

Gold Gloves: 1986, 1987, 1988, 1989, 1991, 1992

Silver Sluggers: 1986, 1987, 1988, 1989, 1992, 1994

BARRY BONDS

Barry Bonds waited on the slow curveball. He then turned his hips and unleashed his powerful swing. Bonds launched the pitch deep into the right-field seats. The San Francisco Giants' outfielder had just hit his seventy-third home run of the 2001 season. That set a new major league record.

Bonds's rise to become the game's best power hitter was controversial. His body changed a lot during his career. So some people think he used steroids to get bigger and stronger. Bonds has never admitted to that, though. Regardless, his home run totals for a season (73) and career (762) remained records through 2013.

The San Francisco Giants' Barry Bonds hits his record seventy-third home run of the 2001 season.

Even before he became the home run king, Bonds was one of the most complete players in baseball history. In 1996, he hit 42 home runs and stole 40 bases. His speed was a big asset on defense, too. Bonds won eight Gold Gloves for his play in left field.

Bonds's father, Bobby, was a major league player, as well. And his godfather was Hall of Famer Willie Mays.

Barry Bonds began his career with the Pittsburgh Pirates. In 1990, he won the NL MVP Award and led the Pirates to the playoffs. He went to the Giants after the 1992 season. And he again was MVP in his first season there. Then from 2001 to 2004, Bonds was the NL MVP four times in a row. That had never happened before.

514

The number of bases Bonds stole during his career. Through 2013, he was the only player in baseball history with more than 500 home runs and more than 500 stolen bases.

"You can't tell me the Babe [Ruth] was any better than this guy," longtime manager Jack McKeon said. "You can't tell me this guy isn't the best player in the history of the game."

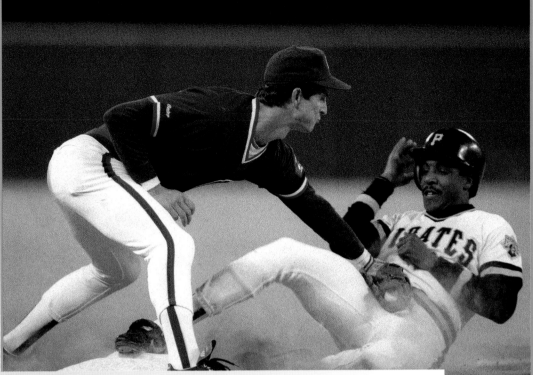

Barry Bonds, then with the Pittsburgh Pirates, safely slides into third during a 1987 game against the Chicago Cubs.

BARRY BONDS

Hometown: Riverside, California

Height, Weight: 6 feet 1, 185 pounds

Birth Date: July 24, 1964

Teams: Pittsburgh Pirates (1986–92)
San Francisco Giants (1993–2007)

All-Star Games: 1990, 1992, 1993, 1994, 1995, 1996, 1997, 1998, 2000, 2001, 2002, 2003, 2004, 2007

Gold Gloves: 1990, 1991, 1992, 1993, 1994, 1996, 1997, 1998

MVP Awards: 1990, 1992, 1993, 2001, 2002, 2003, 2004

Silver Sluggers: 1990, 1991, 1992, 1993, 1994, 1996, 1997, 2000, 2001, 2002, 2003, 2004

KEN GRIFFEY JR.

The ball carried toward the deepest part of Yankee Stadium. Seattle Mariners center fielder Ken Griffey Jr. sprinted toward the fence. He had to run a long, long way. Griffey watched the ball. He glanced at the fence. And then he planted his right cleat into the padded fence and pushed himself upward. With his shoulders at the top of the fence, he stretched out his right arm. Timing his jump perfectly, he caught the ball. He had turned a sure home run into an out.

That is the kind of play that earned Griffey 10 straight Gold Gloves.

When Griffey first became a major leaguer, he was known as "Junior" or "The Kid." That is because his father, Ken Griffey Sr., also played in the majors.

The Seattle Mariners' Ken Griffey Jr. watches a home run head for the stands during a 1995 game.

In 1990, the Griffeys were teammates in Seattle. In one game, they hit back-to-back home runs. Through 2013, they were the only father and son ever to do that in a major league game.

"Junior" had a smooth, powerful left-handed swing. He hit .300 or better eight seasons in the majors. And he hit 630 home runs in his career. Through 2013, that ranked sixth in major league history.

Griffey's best season might have been in 1997. That year, he led the AL in runs (125), home runs (56), and RBIs (147). He was named the AL MVP. However, injuries slowed down Griffey later in his career.

56

Griffey's highest single-season home run total. He hit 56 home runs in 1997 and again in 1998.

"Obviously he had an incredible Hall of Fame career without a doubt," former Oakland Athletics manager Bob Geren said. "One of the best players I've ever played against. Exceptional speed, power, and defense.

Seattle center fielder Ken Griffey Jr. dives to make a catch during a 1996 game against the Boston Red Sox.

KEN GRIFFEY JR.

Hometown: Donora, Pennsylvania

Height, Weight: 6 feet 3, 195 pounds

Birth Date: November 21, 1969

Teams: Seattle Mariners (1989–99, 2009–10)
Cincinnati Reds (2000–08)
Chicago White Sox (2008)

All-Star Games: 1990, 1991, 1992, 1993, 1994, 1995, 1996, 1997, 1998, 1999, 2000, 2004, 2007

Gold Gloves: 1990, 1991, 1992, 1993, 1994, 1995, 1996, 1997, 1997, 1999

MVP Award: 1997

Silver Sluggers: 1991, 1993, 1994, 1996, 1997, 1998, 1999

57

ICHIRO SUZUKI

Ichiro Suzuki had already been a superstar in his native Japan. But in 2001, at age 27, he left Japan and joined the Seattle Mariners. Japanese fans were watching closely. Baseball is very popular in Japan. However, not many Japanese players had made the major leagues. And only a few had done well. Could Suzuki?

He answered that question right away. Suzuki led the AL in batting average (.350), hits (242), and stolen bases (56) in 2001. He was named both the AL Rookie of the Year and the AL MVP.

Suzuki also showed off his powerful arm. In an early-season game, he threw out a base runner at third with a bull's-eye throw from right field. One writer called the throw "a 200-foot lightning bolt." Suzuki won 10 straight Gold Gloves between 2001 and 2010 for his defense in right field.

Seattle Mariners outfielder Ichiro Suzuki hits his 2,500th career hit, including his time in Japan, in 2006.

Suzuki is not a big slugger. Instead, he depends on outstanding hand-eye coordination and blazing speed. He frequently slaps the ball toward left field and shoots out of the batter's box. With his speed, a slow grounder to third base or shortstop is often a hit.

262

The number of hits Suzuki had in 2004, a single-season record. He had at least 200 hits every season from 2001 to 2010.

"You can call some guys' infield hits cheap, but not his. He has amazing technique," said Brandon Inge, then with the Detroit Tigers.

In 2004, Suzuki slapped a ball into center field for his 258th hit of the season. That broke a major league record that had stood for 84 years. Through 2013, Suzuki has led the AL in hits seven times. And he's not done yet. He is proving that he is one of the best outfielders not just in the majors, but in the world.

Seattle's Ichiro Suzuki dives to catch a fly ball against the New York Yankees in 2012.

ICHIRO SUZUKI

Hometown: Kasugai, Japan

Height, Weight: 5 feet 11, 170 pounds

Birth Date: October 22, 1973

Teams: Seattle Mariners (2001–12)
New York Yankees (2012–)

All-Star Games: 2001, 2002, 2003, 2004, 2005, 2006, 2007, 2008, 2009, 2010

Gold Gloves: 2001, 2002, 2003, 2004, 2005, 2006, 2007, 2008, 2009, 2010

MVP Award: 2001

Silver Sluggers: 2001, 2007, 2009

Rookie of the Year: 2001

HONORABLE MENTIONS

James "Cool Papa" Bell – A star in the Negro Leagues in the 1920s and 1930s, Bell is considered one of the fastest players in baseball history. He was an outstanding center fielder as a member of the Pittsburgh Crawfords—perhaps the best team in Negro Leagues history.

Lou Brock – Brock, a longtime St. Louis Cardinals left fielder, had more than 3,000 career hits and was the best base stealer of his generation. He finished his career with 938 steals, which was a record when he retired in 1979.

Andre Dawson – Dawson won the NL Rookie of the Year Award (1977) with the Montreal Expos and the NL MVP Award (1987) with the Chicago Cubs. He also won eight Gold Gloves in a career that spanned 21 seasons.

Tony Gwynn – Gwynn was a five-time Gold Glove winner and one of the best hitters of the 1980s and 1990s. He finished his career with a .338 batting average and won eight batting titles with the San Diego Padres.

Andruw Jones – Jones was the All-Star center fielder on the Atlanta Braves teams that won 10 straight division titles from 1996 to 2005. His total of 10 Gold Gloves tied for second all-time among outfielders through 2013. Jones also hit 434 home runs in his career.

Mel Ott – Ott was a top outfielder and one of the best power hitters of the 1930s and 1940s with the New York Giants. Ott finished his career with 511 home runs—an NL record at the time.

Ted Williams – One of the best hitters in baseball history, Williams covered the outfield in Boston for 19 seasons. He batted .344 for his career, won six batting titles, and twice won the AL Triple Crown (1942, 1947).

Dave Winfield – Winfield totaled 3,110 hits in a career that went from 1973 to 1995 and included six teams. Primarily a right fielder, Winfield won seven Gold Gloves and was a 12-time All-Star.

GLOSSARY

assist
A play in which a defensive player throws a ball that leads to a base runner being called out.

dynasty
A team that wins several championships over a short period of time.

general manager
A team executive who oversees most of the personnel decisions for the team, including trades and signings.

pennant
A long, triangular flag. In baseball, the word is used to describe a league championship.

perfect game
A game in which the pitcher retires all 27 of the opposing players in order, allowing no hits and no walks.

power alley
The areas of a baseball field in left-center field and right-center field.

rookie
A first-year player in the major leagues.

unassisted double play
When one player records two outs all by himself.

FOR MORE INFORMATION

Further Readings

National Baseball Hall of Fame and Museum. *Inside the Baseball Hall of Fame*. New York: Simon & Schuster, 2013.

Sports Illustrated Kids. *Sports Illustrated Kids Full Count: Top 10 Lists of Everything in Baseball*. New York: Time Home Entertainment Inc., 2012.

Web Links

To learn more about MLB's best outfielders, visit ABDO Publishing Company online at **www.abdopublishing.com**. Web sites about MLB's best outfielders are featured on our Book Links page. These links are routinely monitored and updated to provide the most current information available.

INDEX

Aaron, Hank, 26–29
Anaheim Angels, 45
Atlanta Braves, 29

Baltimore Orioles, 30, 34, 36, 37
Bonds, Barry, 50–53
Bonds, Bobby, 52
Boston Red Sox, 6, 9, 38, 41, 45
Brooklyn Dodgers, 14

California Angels, 37
Chicago White Sox, 57
Cincinnati Reds, 34, 36, 37, 57
Clemente, Roberto, 30–33
Cleveland Indians, 8, 9, 18, 37

Detroit Tigers, 6, 22, 24, 25, 60
DiMaggio, Joe, 10–13

Griffey, Ken, Jr., 54–57
Griffey, Ken, Sr., 54, 56

Hall of Fame, 12, 52, 56
Heilmann, Harry, 6
Henderson, Rickey, 42–45

Kaline, Al, 22–25

Larsen, Don, 14
Los Angeles Dodgers, 37, 45

Mantle, Mickey, 14–17
Mays, Willie, 18–21, 52
Milwaukee Braves, 26, 29
Milwaukee Brewers, 29
Minnesota Twins, 38, 46, 48, 49
Musial, Stan, 12

Negro Leagues, 20, 26
New York Giants, 10, 18, 20, 21
New York Mets, 21, 45
New York Yankees, 10, 12, 13, 14, 16, 17, 26, 45, 54, 61

Oakland Athletics, 44, 45, 56

Pittsburgh Pirates, 30, 33, 52, 53
Puckett, Kirby, 46–49

Robinson, Frank, 34–37

San Diego Padres, 45
San Francisco Giants, 21, 50, 52, 53
Seattle Mariners, 45, 54, 57, 58, 61
Selig, Bud (commissioner), 28
Speaker, Tris, 6–9
Suzuki, Ichiro, 58–61

Toronto Blue Jays, 44, 45

Washington Senators, 9
Wertz, Vic, 18
White, Bill, 20

Yastrzemski, Carl, 38–41

ABOUT THE AUTHOR

Bo Smolka is a former sports copy editor at the *Baltimore Sun* and former sports information director at Bucknell University, his alma mater. He has won several national writing awards, including the National Story of the Year from the College Sports Information Directors of America. He lives in Baltimore, Maryland, with his wife and two children. When he is not writing about baseball, he can often be found coaching his son's baseball teams.